10 - WEEK DEVOTIONS FOR GRANDMA

A GRANDMA PRAYER AND GIFT BOOK

HEARTFELT SCRIPTURES, PRAYERS, AND REFLECTIONS OF A JOYFUL SEASON

Best grandma ever

DR. FANATOMY
★★★★★

copyright@ dr. fanatomy 2024

All rights reserved. No part of this publication may be reproduced, distributed, or transmitted in any form or by any means, including photocopying, recording, or other electronic or mechanical methods, without the prior written permission of the publisher, except in the case of brief quotations embodied in critical reviews and certain other noncommercial uses permitted by copyright law.

This book is a work of non-fiction, and any resemblance to actual persons, living or dead, or actual events is purely coincidental.

The information and techniques described in this book are intended for educational and informational purposes only. The author and publisher shall not be held liable for any injury, damage, or loss arising from using or misusing the information presented in this book.

While every effort has been made to ensure the accuracy of the information contained within this book, the author and publisher make no warranties or representations express or implied, about the completeness, accuracy, reliability, suitability, or availability with respect to the contents of this book for any purpose. The use of any information provided in this book is at the reader's own risk.

TABLE OF CONTENTS

1. INTRODUCTION (Pg: 1-7)

- **Welcome Message**: *A personal greeting for grandmothers, explaining the purpose of the book. Encouragement for grandmothers to embrace their spiritual journey and the influence they hold in their families.*
- **How to Use This Book**: *Brief guidance on how the book is designed for a quick, meaningful daily devotion.*
- **The Role of Grandmothers in the Family**: *A reflection on the unique and powerful influence grandmothers have in the lives of their families, offering wisdom and love.*
- **A Prayer for Grandmothers**: *A special prayer asking for peace, joy, and blessings as grandmothers continue their important role.*

2. WEEK 1: PREPARING YOUR HEART (THEME: EMBRACING PEACE)
(Pg: 8-15)

- **Devotion 1: The Peace That Comes from Faith**
    - *Scripture: Isaiah 9:6*
    - *Reflection: The promise of peace through a relationship with God.*
    - *Prayer: A prayer for inner peace in daily life.*
    - *Affirmation: "I welcome God's peace into my heart."*

- **Devotion 2: Finding Rest in God's Presence**
    - *Scripture: Matthew 11:28*
    - *Reflection: Resting in God's peace amid life's busyness.*
    - *Prayer: A prayer for quiet moments with God.*
    - *Affirmation: "I find rest in the presence of the Lord."*

- **Devotion 3: Letting Go of Worry**
    - *Scripture: Philippians 4:6-7*
    - *Reflection: Trusting God with every worry, big or small.*
    - *Prayer: A prayer of surrender, releasing worries to God.*
    - *Affirmation: "I trust in God's care for me."*

- **Devotion 4: Peace in Family Bonds**
    - *Scripture: Colossians 3:15*
    - *Reflection: Reflecting on the peace that comes with strong family relationships.*
    - *Prayer: A prayer for peace in family dynamics.*
    - *Affirmation: "I foster peace and unity in my family."*

3. WEEK 2: JOY IN EVERYDAY LIFE (THEME: EMBRACING JOY)
(Pg: 16-24)

- **Devotion 5: The Joy of Faith**
    - *Scripture: Luke 2:10-11*
    - *Reflection: Celebrating the joy that comes with faith.*
    - *Prayer: A prayer of joy and thanksgiving for spiritual blessings.*
    - *Affirmation: "I celebrate the joy of my faith."*

- **Devotion 6: Joy in Family Gatherings**
    - *Scripture: Psalm 133:1*
    - *Reflection: Finding joy in shared moments and traditions with family.*
    - *Prayer: A prayer of gratitude for family connections.*
    - *Affirmation: "I cherish joyful moments with my family."*

- **Devotion 7: The Gift of Laughter**
    - *Scripture: Proverbs 17:22*
    - *Reflection: The healing power of laughter and joy, even in tough times.*
    - *Prayer: A prayer for joy and laughter in the home.*
    - *Affirmation: "I embrace laughter as a gift from God."*

- **Devotion 8: Rejoicing in God's Blessings**
    - *Scripture: James 1:17*
    - *Reflection: Acknowledging the many blessings God has given.*
    - *Prayer: A prayer of thankfulness for life's gifts.*
    - *Affirmation: "I rejoice in the blessings God has given me."*

4. WEEK 3: GIVING AND GRATITUDE (THEME: EMBRACING GENEROSITY)

(Pg: 25-33)

- **Devotion 9: The Gift of Giving**
    - *Scripture: 2 Corinthians 9:7*
    - *Reflection: Finding joy in giving, not just receiving.*
    - *Prayer: A prayer of thanksgiving for the opportunity to give to others.*
    - *Affirmation: "I find joy in giving generously."*

- **Devotion 10: Gratitude for the Little Things**
    - *Scripture: 1 Thessalonians 5:16-18*
    - *Reflection: Reflecting on the small gifts and joys in life that are easy to overlook.*
    - *Prayer: A prayer of thanks for life's simple gifts.*
    - *Affirmation: "I am thankful for the simple gifts God provides."*

- **Devotion 11: Grateful for Family**
    - *Scripture: Ephesians 5:20*
    - *Reflection: Focusing on gratitude for family and the relationships that sustain us.*
    - *Prayer: A prayer of gratitude for the love of family.*
    - *Affirmation: "I am thankful for my family and their love."*

- **Devotion 12: Grateful for God's Provision**
    - *Scripture: Philippians 4:19*
    - *Reflection: Trusting that God provides everything we need, even in challenging times.*
    - *Prayer: A prayer for continued provision.*
    - *Affirmation: "I trust in God's provision for my life."*

5. WEEK 4: REFLECTING ON GOD'S PRESENCE (THEME: EMBRACING FAITH)

(Pg: 34-42)

- **Devotion 13: The Humility of Jesus**
    - *Scripture: Luke 2:7*
    - *Reflection: Embracing humility in our own lives.*
    - *Prayer: A prayer asking for humility in our hearts and homes.*
    - *Affirmation: "I embrace the humble heart of Jesus."*

- **Devotion 14: The Light of God**
  - *Scripture: John 8:12*
  - *Reflection: God as the light of the world and how we can reflect His light.*
  - *Prayer: A prayer for God's light to shine in your life.*
  - *Affirmation: "I am a reflection of God's light."*

- **Devotion 15: God, Our Savior**
  - *Scripture: Matthew 1:21*
  - *Reflection: Rejoicing in God's saving grace.*
  - *Prayer: A prayer of thankfulness for the salvation God offers.*
  - *Affirmation: "I rejoice in the salvation God brings."*

- **Devotion 16: God, Our Peace**
  - *Scripture: Ephesians 2:14*
  - *Reflection: The peace that God brings to our hearts and homes.*
  - *Prayer: A prayer for peace in daily life.*
  - *Affirmation: "I receive the peace God offers."*

6. WEEK 5: REFLECTING ON GRATITUDE AND LOVE (THEME: CELEBRATING GOD'S GIFTS)

(Pg: 43 -50)

- **Devotion 17: The Gift of Life**
  - *Scripture: Psalm 139:14*
  - *Reflection: Reflecting on the miracle of life and the joy it brings.*
  - *Prayer: A prayer of joy and reverence for the gift of life.*
  - *Affirmation: "I celebrate the gift of life."*

- **Devotion 18: The Gift of Love**
  - *Scripture: John 3:16*
  - *Reflection: God's ultimate gift to us is love.*
  - *Prayer: A prayer for the love of God to fill your heart and home.*
  - *Affirmation: "I embrace God's love in my life."*

- **Devotion 19: Hope in God's Promises**
  - *Scripture: Romans 15:13*
  - *Reflection: Finding hope in God's promises.*
  - *Prayer: A prayer for hope and joy in everyday life.*
  - *Affirmation: "I carry the hope of God in my heart."*

7. WEEK 6: STRENGTH THROUGH CHALLENGES (THEME: FINDING RESILIENCE IN FAITH)

(Pg: 51 -58)

- **Devotion 20: Leaning on God in Difficult Times**
  - *Scripture: Psalm 46:1*
  - *Reflection: Trusting God as our refuge and strength during life's storms.*
  - *Prayer: A prayer for courage and resilience through challenges.*
  - *Affirmation: "I am strong through God's unwavering support."*

- **Devotion 21: Finding Peace Amid Uncertainty**
  - *Scripture: Isaiah 41:10*
  - *Reflection: Resting in God's promise to never leave us.*
  - *Prayer: A prayer for calm and clarity in times of doubt.*
  - *Affirmation: "I am secure in God's constant presence."*

- **Devotion 22: Trusting God's Timing**
  - *Scripture: Ecclesiastes 3:1*
  - *Reflection: Patience in waiting for God's perfect plan to unfold.*
  - *Prayer: A prayer for faith and trust in God's timing.*
  - *Affirmation: "I trust God's plan for my life."*

8. WEEK 7: PASSING DOWN FAITH (THEME: CREATING A SPIRITUAL LEGACY)

(Pg: 59 -66)

- **Devotion 23: Sharing God's Love with the Next Generation**
  - *Scripture: Deuteronomy 6:6-7*
  - *Reflection: Teaching and modeling faith to grandchildren and family.*
  - *Prayer: A prayer for wisdom in guiding the younger generation spiritually.*
  - *Affirmation: "I leave a legacy of love and faith."*

- **Devotion 24: The Power of a Praying Grandmother**
  - *Scripture: James 5:16*
  - *Reflection: How intercessory prayer impacts family lives.*
  - *Prayer: A prayer for strength and guidance as a prayer warrior.*
  - *Affirmation: "My prayers uplift and protect my family."*

- **Devotion 25: Planting Seeds of Faith**
  - *Scripture: Galatians 6:9*
  - *Reflection: Trusting that small acts of love and faith will bear fruit in time.*
  - *Prayer: A prayer for perseverance in nurturing faith in others.*
  - *Affirmation: "I plant seeds of faith that will grow for generations."*

9. WEEK 8: EMBRACING GOD'S PROMISES (THEME: LIVING IN GOD'S FAITHFULNESS)

(Pg: 67 - 74)

- **Devotion 26: God's Faithfulness Through Every Season**
  - *Scripture: Lamentations 3:22-23*
  - *Reflection: Finding comfort in the unchanging faithfulness of God.*
  - *Prayer: A prayer of thanksgiving for God's enduring promises.*
  - *Affirmation: "I trust in God's faithfulness through all seasons."*

- **Devotion 27: Rejoicing in Eternal Life**
  - *Scripture: John 14:2-3*
  - *Reflection: The hope and assurance of God's eternal promise.*
  - *Prayer: A prayer of gratitude for the gift of salvation and eternal life.*
  - *Affirmation: "I look forward to the eternal joy God has promised."*

- **Devotion 28: God's Plan for Good**
  - *Scripture: Jeremiah 29:11*
  - *Reflection: Trusting in God's plans for a hopeful and fulfilling future.*
  - *Prayer: A prayer for wisdom and strength to follow God's path.*
  - *Affirmation: "I walk confidently in the plans God has for me."*

10. WEEK 9: WALKING IN OBEDIENCE (THEME: ALIGNING YOUR LIFE WITH GOD'S WILL)

(Pg: 75 -84)

- **Devotion 29: Listening to God's Voice**
  - *Scripture: John 10:27*
  - *Reflection: Recognizing and responding to the voice of God in your daily life.*
  - *Prayer: A prayer for discernment and clarity to hear God's guidance.*
  - *Affirmation: "I listen for God's voice and follow His lead."*

- **Devotion 30: The Blessings of Obedience**
  - *Scripture: Deuteronomy 28:1-2*
  - *Reflection: How obedience to God's Word brings blessings to your life and family.*
  - *Prayer: A prayer for strength and dedication to follow God's commands.*
  - *Affirmation: "I am blessed as I walk in obedience to God."*

- **Devotion 31: Trusting in God's Commands**
  - *Scripture: Proverbs 3:5-6*
  - *Reflection: Trusting in God's ways even when they challenge your understanding.*
  - *Prayer: A prayer for faith to trust in God's perfect plan.*
  - *Affirmation: "I trust in the Lord and lean on His understanding."*

- **Devotion 32: Obedience in Daily Living**
  - *Scripture: Psalm 119:105*
  - *Reflection: Letting God's Word be the guide in every aspect of life.*
  - *Prayer: A prayer for focus and courage to live in God's light.*
  - *Affirmation: "God's Word lights my path as I walk in obedience."*

11. WEEK 10: THE POWER (THEME: RELEASING BURDENS THROUGH GRACE)

(Pg: 85 - 92)

- **Devotion 33: Forgiving as God Forgives**
  - *Scripture: Colossians 3:13*
  - *Reflection: Reflecting on the example of Christ's forgiveness and its transformative power.*
  - *Prayer: A prayer for grace to forgive as you have been forgiven.*
  - *Affirmation: "I forgive others as God has forgiven me."*

- **Devotion 34: Finding Freedom in Forgiveness**
  - *Scripture: Matthew 6:14-15*
  - *Reflection: Letting go of anger and resentment to embrace the freedom of forgiveness.*
  - *Prayer: A prayer for strength to release past hurts and embrace healing.*
  - *Affirmation: "Forgiveness brings peace and freedom to my soul."*

- **Devotion 35: Restoring Broken Relationships**
  - *Scripture: Romans 12:18*
  - *Reflection: Taking steps to mend relationships and live in harmony with others.*
  - *Prayer: A prayer for wisdom and courage to seek reconciliation.*
  - *Affirmation: "I seek peace and restoration in all my relationships."*

CONCLUSION

(Pg: 93)

APPENDIX

(Pg: 94 - 96)

1. Introduction

Embracing the Festive Season with Heart and Hope

Dear Grandma,

Welcome to this special prayer book, lovingly created to support and uplift you on your spiritual journey. Whether you're a new grandmother or have spent years enjoying the blessing of grandchildren, this book is a reflection of the unique role you hold in your family and your vital connection to God.

As a grandmother, you embody wisdom, love, and patience. Your family looks up to you for guidance, and your spiritual strength radiates through your words and actions. This book was created to help you nurture that spiritual connection—both with God and your loved ones. You play a key role in shaping the faith and values of your family, and through your prayers, you pass on a spiritual legacy that will bless generations to come.

This prayer book is designed to be a companion on your journey, offering moments of peace, reflection, and encouragement. In a world that can often be fast-paced and chaotic, it's essential to carve out time to center your heart in God's presence, whether for a few minutes in the morning or during quiet moments throughout the day. Through this book, I hope you find inspiration and comfort in knowing that your prayers, your faith, and your love are deeply impactful to your family and pleasing to God.
May this book remind you of the precious gifts you have—both the blessings you give and receive as a grandmother—and how central your role is in the lives of those you love. Let it also be a source of strength for you as you continue your spiritual walk, helping you embrace the grace and wisdom that come from your relationship with God.

With love,

....

How to Use This Book

This prayer book is designed to be simple and flexible, allowing you to find comfort and strength whenever you need it. Each devotion is brief but meaningful, providing a daily moment to connect with God and reflect on the blessings of life as a grandmother.

Each day, you will find:

- **Scripture**: A passage from the Bible to anchor the day's reflection.
- **Reflection**: A short message or thought designed to encourage and uplift you.
- **Prayer**: A guided prayer that you can say aloud or in your heart, asking for God's guidance and blessings.
- **Affirmation:** A simple statement of faith that you can carry with you throughout the day, reminding you of God's presence.

You can use this book in the way that works best for you—whether it's reading a devotion every morning, meditating on a scripture before bed, or turning to it whenever you feel the need for encouragement. There's no right or wrong way to use it; the purpose is to create moments where you feel connected to God and reminded of His love for you.

At the back of the book, there are additional blank pages for your personal thoughts, prayers, and reflections. These pages are yours to use as you wish—to jot down insights, special prayers, or even to write letters to your loved ones. Over time, you may find that these personal notes become part of your family's legacy as well.

The Role of Grandmothers in the Family

Being a grandmother is a privilege, a sacred calling. You are a bridge between generations, a keeper of traditions, and a beacon of love and wisdom. Your influence, whether near or far, shapes the lives of your grandchildren in profound ways.

You offer a safe haven, a listening ear, and a comforting embrace. Your prayers, your words of encouragement, and your unwavering love nurture their souls. You instill values, share stories, and pass down traditions, creating a legacy that will last for generations.

In a world that often feels chaotic and uncertain, your presence is a constant source of peace and stability. Your gentle guidance, your quiet strength, and your unwavering faith inspire those around you.

This book is a tribute to the incredible role you play. It's a tool to help you deepen your own spiritual journey, so that you can continue to bless your family with love, wisdom, and faith. May your journey as a grandmother be filled with joy, peace, and the fulfillment of knowing you've made a lasting impact.

A Prayer for Grandmothers

Heavenly Father,

I come before You with a heart full of gratitude for the gift of being a grandmother. Thank You for the joy that my family brings me, for the moments of laughter, love, and shared memories. Thank You for the opportunity to offer wisdom and guidance to my children and grandchildren, and for the role You've given me as a spiritual leader in my family.

Lord, I ask for Your continued blessing over me as I fulfill this role. Grant me patience when challenges arise, strength when I feel weary, and wisdom to know how best to guide those I love. Help me to be a source of peace, love, and joy in my family, reflecting Your grace in all that I do.

Please bless my family—each child, grandchild, and great-grandchild—with Your protection, peace, and love. Help me to encourage them in their faith and be a steadfast presence in their lives. Let me be an example of Your unfailing love.

Thank You for the privilege of being a grandmother. Continue to walk beside me and give me the grace to fulfill this sacred role with joy and faithfulness.

In Jesus' name, Amen.

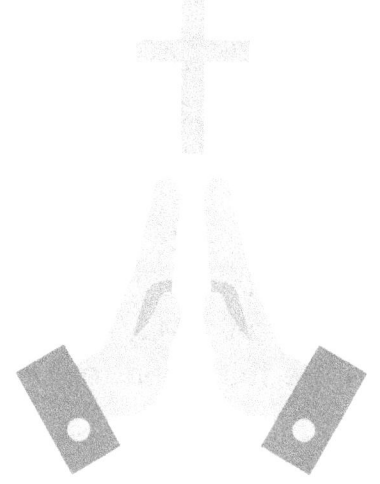

Activity for you

Take a few quiet moments to reflect on your journey as a grandmother. Write a personal letter to your grandchildren, sharing your thoughts, wisdom, and prayers for them. In your letter, consider including:

- *A special memory you have with them that brought you joy.*
- *Any advice or life lessons you want them to carry with them as they grow.*
- *A personal prayer or blessing that you ask God to give them as they navigate life's challenges.*

Feel free to write from the heart, and let your love and faith shine through your words. This letter could become a treasured keepsake for your grandchildren, a reminder of your love and the spiritual legacy you're passing on.

Week 1: Preparing Your Heart

Theme: Embracing Peace

Devotion 1: The Peace That Comes from Faith

Scripture: Isaiah 9:6

"For to us a child is born, to us a son is given, and the government will be on his shoulders. And he will be called Wonderful Counselor, Mighty God, Everlasting Father, Prince of Peace."

Reflection:

The promise of peace through a relationship with God is a gift beyond measure. As we look to Jesus, the Prince of Peace, we are reminded that His peace is always available, even in the most challenging times.

- **Think about a moment in your life when you felt God's peace was over you**

....

....

....

- **What does God's peace mean to you?**

....

....

Prayer:

Heavenly Father, I thank You for the peace that only You can provide. Fill my heart with Your peace today, and help me to trust in You no matter what challenges I face. May Your peace calm my worries and bring me comfort in all circumstances.
 In Jesus' name, I pray, Amen.

Affirmation:

"I welcome God's peace into my heart."

Devotion 2: Finding Rest in God's Presence

Scripture: Matthew 11:28

"Come to me, all you who are weary and burdened, and I will give you rest."

Reflection:

Life can sometimes feel overwhelming with all its busyness and responsibilities. But in God's presence, we can find true rest. He invites us to come to Him, lay down our burdens, and experience His peace.

- **When was the last time you felt truly at rest in God's presence?**

....

....

....

- **How can you create more quiet moments to spend with God?**

....

....

Prayer:

Lord, help me find rest in Your presence. In the busyness of life, draw me closer to You, and remind me to take moments to pause and be still. Grant me the peace that comes from resting in You, both physically and spiritually. In Jesus' name, Amen.

Affirmation:

"I find rest in the presence of the Lord."

Devotion 3 Letting Go of Worry

Scripture : Philippians 4:6-7

"Do not be anxious about anything, but in every situation, by prayer and petition, with thanksgiving, present your requests to God. And the peace of God, which transcends all understanding, will guard your hearts and your minds in Christ Jesus."

Reflection:

Worry can weigh heavily on our hearts. But God calls us to release our worries to Him, trusting that He is in control. As we surrender our concerns, He grants us peace beyond understanding.

- **What is something you've been worrying about lately?**

....

....

- **How can you release this worry to God?**

....

....

Prayer:

Dear God, I bring my worries and fears to You today. I surrender them into Your capable hands, knowing that You care for me and have a perfect plan for my life. Replace my worry with Your peace, and help me to trust in Your guidance. In Jesus' name, Amen.

Affirmation:

"I trust in God's care for me."

Devotion 4 : Peace in Family Bonds

Scripture : Colossians 3:15

"Let the peace of Christ rule in your hearts, since as members of one body you were called to peace. And be thankful."

Reflection:

Family relationships can be one of the greatest sources of joy and, at times, challenge. Yet, God desires for peace to reign in our families. By fostering love, forgiveness, and understanding, we contribute to the unity and peace within our homes.

- **Think of a time when your family experienced peace and harmony. What contributed to that peace?**

....

....

- **What steps can you take to bring more peace into your family today?**

....

....

Prayer:

Father, I pray for peace in my family. Help us to love one another deeply, forgive freely, and always seek to understand one another. May Your peace rule in our hearts and our home, strengthening the bond between us. In Jesus' name, Amen.

Affirmation:

"I foster peace and unity in my family."

By reflecting on these devotions, taking time to pray, and filling in the personal reflections, you are preparing your heart to embrace God's peace in all areas of your life.

Activity for You: Embracing Peace

Take a moment to reflect on the peace that God has brought into your life. Write a personal letter to yourself or to a loved one about your journey towards peace. Consider including the following:
- *A time in your life when you experienced God's peace in a difficult situation.*
- *What helps you find rest in God's presence when life feels overwhelming?*
- *How do you let go of worries and trust God's plan?*
- *What are your hopes and prayers for peace within your family and in the lives of your grandchildren?*

Let your words flow from the heart, and remember that your reflections on peace can offer wisdom and comfort to those you love. Write about how embracing peace has shaped your spiritual journey and the role it plays in your family.

Week 2: Joy in Everyday Life
Theme: Embracing Joy

Devotion 5 : The Joy of Faith

Scripture: Luke 2:10-11

"But the angel said to them, 'Do not be afraid. I bring you good news that will cause great joy for all the people. Today in the town of David a Savior has been born to you; he is the Messiah, the Lord.'"

Reflection:

Faith brings a deep and abiding joy that transcends circumstances. The birth of Jesus was a moment of great joy, not only for those who witnessed it but for all of humanity. This joy is still present for us today, as our faith in God brings us peace, hope, and a sense of purpose. When we reflect on our faith, we tap into a joy that can sustain us through all of life's challenges.

- **How does your faith bring you joy? Write your thoughts here:**

....

....

....

....

- **Write down a moment when your faith brought you joy:**

....

....

....

Prayer:

Dear Lord, I thank You for the joy that comes from knowing You. Help me to always remember the good news of Your love and salvation, and let my heart be filled with joy. No matter what I face, may I find strength and happiness in the knowledge that You are always with me. Amen.

Affirmation:

"I celebrate the joy of my faith."

Devotion 6 : Joy in Family Gatherings

Scripture: Psalm 133:1

"How good and pleasant it is when God's people live together in unity!"

Reflection:

Family gatherings are a source of joy and celebration. Whether it's a large holiday gathering or a small meal together, the time spent with family strengthens bonds and creates lasting memories. Family traditions, laughter, and shared stories are blessings that we should cherish. These moments remind us of the importance of unity and love within the family.

- **Think about a recent family gathering that brought you joy. What made it special? Reflect on it here:**

....

....

....

Prayer:

Lord, I thank You for the gift of family. Help me to always appreciate the joy that comes from spending time with loved ones. May our family gatherings be filled with love, unity, and gratitude for all the blessings You have given us. Amen.

Affirmation:

I cherish joyful moments with my family.

- **Write about a joyful memory with your family that you want to remember forever:**

....

....

....

....

Devotion 7 : The Gift of Laughter

Scripture : Proverbs 17:22

"A cheerful heart is good medicine, but a crushed spirit dries up the bones."

Reflection:

Laughter is a gift that lifts our spirits and brings healing to the heart. Even in difficult times, a shared laugh can ease tension and remind us of the goodness of life. Laughter has the power to bring families together and to create an atmosphere of joy. It is a reflection of the light-heartedness that God wants us to experience in our lives..

- **Think of a time when laughter helped you through a tough moment. Reflect on that memory here:**

....

....

....

....

Prayer:

Dear God, thank You for the gift of laughter. Help me to embrace joy and laughter in all circumstances. Let my home be filled with moments of light-heartedness, even in the midst of challenges, and may laughter be a reminder of Your goodness. Amen.

Affirmation:

I embrace laughter as a gift from God.

- **Write about a moment when laughter brought healing or comfort to you or someone in your family:**

....

....

....

....

....

Devotion 8 : Rejoicing in God's Blessings

Scripture: James 1:17

"Every good and perfect gift is from above, coming down from the Father of the heavenly lights, who does not change like shifting shadows."

Reflection:

We are surrounded by blessings every day, both big and small. From the love of family to the beauty of nature, every good thing in our lives is a gift from God. Taking time to acknowledge and rejoice in these blessings helps us to cultivate a spirit of gratitude. Rejoicing in God's blessings reminds us that even in the midst of challenges, there is always something to be thankful for.

- **List three blessings you are grateful for today:**

....

....

....

....

- **Write about a blessing that you are especially thankful for today:**

....

....

....

....

Prayer:

Heavenly Father, thank You for the countless blessings You have given me. Help me to always recognize Your goodness in my life and to rejoice in every blessing, no matter how small. May I carry a heart of gratitude and joy, and share that joy with others. Amen.

Affirmation:

I rejoice in the blessings God has given me.

Activity for You: Joy in Everyday Life

Take a moment to reflect on the joy you've experienced throughout your life as a grandmother. In a letter to your grandchildren, share with them the different ways you find joy in everyday life. Consider including the following in your letter:

1. *A special family tradition or gathering that fills you with joy.*
2. *A memory where laughter brought healing or happiness to your family.*
3. *The blessings in your life that you are most grateful for, and how these blessings remind you of God's goodness.*
4. *Words of encouragement for your grandchildren to embrace joy, even in difficult times.*

Let your letter be a heartfelt expression of the joy you find in faith, family, laughter, and blessings. This could be a beautiful way to share your love and inspire them to seek joy in their own lives.

Week 3: Giving and Gratitude
Theme: Embracing Generosity

Devotion 9 : The Gift of Giving

Scripture: 2 Corinthians 9:7

"Each of you should give what you have decided in your heart to give, not reluctantly or under compulsion, for God loves a cheerful giver."

Reflection:

There is immense joy in giving, whether it's a small token of kindness or a large gift. The act of giving creates a connection between the giver and the receiver, and it brings both closer to God's love. As a grandmother, you know the joy that comes from giving to your family—your time, wisdom, love, and even material gifts. Reflect on how giving has brought you closer to your loved ones. What moments of generosity have filled your heart with joy? How have you felt God's presence when you gave freely and joyfully, expecting nothing in return?

- **What does giving generously mean to you?**

....

....

....

....

- **How have you experienced joy through giving to others?**

....

....

....

....

Prayer:

Dear Lord, thank You for the opportunities You provide me to give. Help me to give with a joyful heart, knowing that every act of kindness reflects Your love. Guide me in sharing my blessings with those around me. Amen.

Affirmation:

"I find joy in giving generously."

Devotion 10: Gratitude for the Little Things

"Rejoice always, pray continually, give thanks in all circumstances; for this is God's will for you in Christ Jesus." – 1 Thessalonians 5:16-18

Reflection:

Life is full of small blessings that are easy to overlook in the busyness of daily life. The warmth of the sun on your face, a smile from a loved one, a moment of peace in the day—these are God's gifts that bring joy if we pause to appreciate them. Reflect on the small, everyday joys that you might sometimes take for granted. What simple pleasures bring you happiness? How can you cultivate a heart of gratitude for these little things? Gratitude transforms the ordinary into something extraordinary, and by focusing on these small gifts, you will experience God's presence in your life in new ways.

- **What small blessings are you grateful for today?**

....

....

....

Prayer:

Heavenly Father, thank You for the countless small blessings that fill my life each day. Help me to notice and appreciate each one, and to always have a heart full of gratitude. May I live in constant awareness of Your goodness. Amen.

Affirmation:

"I am thankful for the simple gifts God provides."

- **Write about a joyful memory with your family that you want to remember forever: How does recognizing these simple joys impact your outlook on life?**

....

....

....

....

Devotion 11 : Grateful for Family

Scripture : Ephesians 5:20

"Always giving thanks to God the Father for everything, in the name of our Lord Jesus Christ."

Reflection:

Family is one of life's greatest blessings. Through all the ups and downs, the love and support of family can be a constant source of strength and joy. As a grandmother, you have seen your family grow, change, and flourish. Reflect on the relationships within your family—your children, grandchildren, and extended family..

What moments of love, care, and togetherness stand out in your mind? How has your family been a source of joy, and how have you expressed gratitude for their presence in your life? Consider how family bonds are a reflection of God's unconditional love for us.

- **What makes you most grateful for your family?**

....

....

....

....

Prayer:

Lord, I thank You for the gift of family. Help me to always appreciate and cherish the love and connection that we share. Give me the strength and wisdom to continue supporting and nurturing my family with grace and kindness. Amen.

Affirmation:

"I am thankful for my family and their love."

- **How do you nurture gratitude within your family relationships?**

....

....

....

....

Devotion 12 : Grateful for God's Provision

Scripture: Philippians 4:19

"And my God will meet all your needs according to the riches of His glory in Christ Jesus."

Reflection:

God is faithful and provides for our needs, even in times of uncertainty. His provision may come in unexpected ways, but it is always timely and abundant. Reflect on the ways God has provided for you throughout your life—spiritually, emotionally, and physically. Have there been moments when you worried about your needs, only to see God's hand at work? How does trusting in God's provision bring you peace, even when life feels uncertain? By recognizing God's faithfulness, you can cultivate a deeper sense of gratitude and trust in His care for you and your loved ones.

- **How has God provided for you in times of need?**

....

....

....

....

- **How can you trust more fully in His provision, even during challenging seasons?**

....

....

Prayer:

Dear Lord, thank You for providing for all my needs, even when I cannot always see Your plan. Help me to trust in Your provision and to know that You are always with me, guiding my steps. Strengthen my faith and fill my heart with gratitude for Your constant care. Amen.

Affirmation:

"I trust in God's provision for my life."

Activity for You: Giving and Gratitude

Take a moment to reflect on the ways you've experienced both giving and gratitude throughout your life.

Write a letter to your grandchildren sharing a story about a time when giving brought you unexpected joy—whether it was a small act of kindness or a larger gesture of generosity. Then, describe a moment when you felt deep gratitude for the simple things in life, such as a family gathering, a peaceful morning, or an answered prayer.

Encourage your grandchildren to embrace the importance of both giving and being grateful, and share the lessons you've learned about how these acts have deepened your faith and brought you closer to God. Let them know how much they mean to you and how thankful you are for the love and joy they bring to your life.

Week 4: Reflecting on God's Presence
Theme: Embracing Faith

Devotion 13 : The Humility of Jesus

Scripture: Luke 2:7

"And she gave birth to her firstborn son and wrapped him in swaddling cloths and laid him in a manger, because there was no room for them in the inn."

Reflection:

The birth of Jesus in such humble circumstances reminds us of the importance of humility. Just as Jesus entered the world in the simplest of settings, we too are called to live humbly, recognizing the value of love, kindness, and service over material wealth or status. Humility is not about thinking less of ourselves but about thinking of ourselves less. How can we show humility in our daily lives and in our relationships with others?

- **Think of a time when you had to set aside your pride to serve others.**

....

....

....

....

- **How has humility shaped your relationships with your family or others?**

....

....

....

....

Prayer:

Dear Lord, help me to cultivate humility in my heart. Just as Jesus was born in a humble manger, guide me to live with a humble spirit, serving others with love and compassion. Teach me to put others first and to find joy in simple acts of kindness. Amen.

Affirmation:

"I embrace the humble heart of Jesus."

Devotion 14 : The Light of God

"I am the light of the world. Whoever follows me will not walk in darkness, but will have the light of life."– John 8:12

Reflection:

Jesus is the light that shines in our darkness, guiding us through difficult times. Just as the sun lights up the world, God's presence brings clarity, hope, and direction to our lives. As grandmothers, you have a unique opportunity to reflect God's light to your family and community. How can you shine His light through your words and actions today?

- **Recall a time when God's light led you out of a dark or difficult situation.**

....

....

....

....

Prayer:

Lord, let your light shine in my life. Fill me with Your presence so that I may reflect Your love, kindness, and grace to everyone I encounter. Help me to be a beacon of hope and faith to my family. Amen.

Affirmation:

"I am a reflection of God's light."

- **How do you reflect God's light in your home, with your grandchildren?**

....

....

....

Devotion 15: God, Our Savior

Scripture : Matthew 1:21

"She will give birth to a son, and you are to give him the name Jesus, because he will save his people from their sins."

Reflection:

Rejoice in the gift of salvation! God sent Jesus into the world to save us, offering us forgiveness, grace, and eternal life. His love for us is unconditional and everlasting. As we reflect on this saving grace, we are reminded of the depth of God's love and the hope we have in Him. How can you share the joy of this salvation with others, especially with your family?

- **What does salvation mean to you personally?**

....

....

....

....

Prayer:

Dear Lord, thank You for the gift of salvation. I am grateful for Your love and grace that covers me. Help me to live in the joy and freedom of Your saving grace, and give me the courage to share this good news with my family and those around me. Amen.

Affirmation:

"I rejoice in the salvation God brings."

- **How can you express your gratitude for God's grace in your daily life?**

....

....

....

....

....

....

Devotion 16 : God, Our Peace

Scripture: Ephesians 2:14

"For He Himself is our peace, who has made the two groups one and has destroyed the barrier, the dividing wall of hostility."

Reflection:

God is the source of true peace, a peace that surpasses all understanding. In our chaotic world, we often find ourselves struggling to find peace amidst the noise and worries of daily life. But God's peace is available to us if we open our hearts to Him. Whether in our homes, relationships, or personal challenges, we can rest in the peace that only God provides. How can you invite God's peace into your life and share it with your family?

- **Think of a situation where you needed God's peace.**

....

....

....

....

- **How do you create an atmosphere of peace in your home?**

....

....

....

Prayer:

Lord, You are the source of peace. I ask for Your peace to fill my heart and my home. Help me to trust in Your presence and to be a calming presence in the lives of my family. May Your peace guard my heart in every situation. Amen.

Affirmation:

"I receive the peace God offers."

Activity for You : Reflecting on God's Presence

Take some time to write a letter to your grandchildren, sharing how God's presence has impacted your life. Reflect on moments when you felt God's peace, His light, and His saving grace. You might want to include:

- A story about a time when you had to rely on God's peace to get through a difficult moment.
- How you've experienced God's light guiding you, even in the darkest of times.
- Your thoughts on the gift of salvation and how you hope your grandchildren will experience the joy of faith in their own lives.
- A prayer or blessing for them, asking God to always be with them and guide them in their journey of faith.

Let your love and faith shine through your words, leaving a spiritual legacy for your grandchildren to treasure.

Week 5: Reflecting on Gratitude and Love

Theme: Celebrating God's Gifts

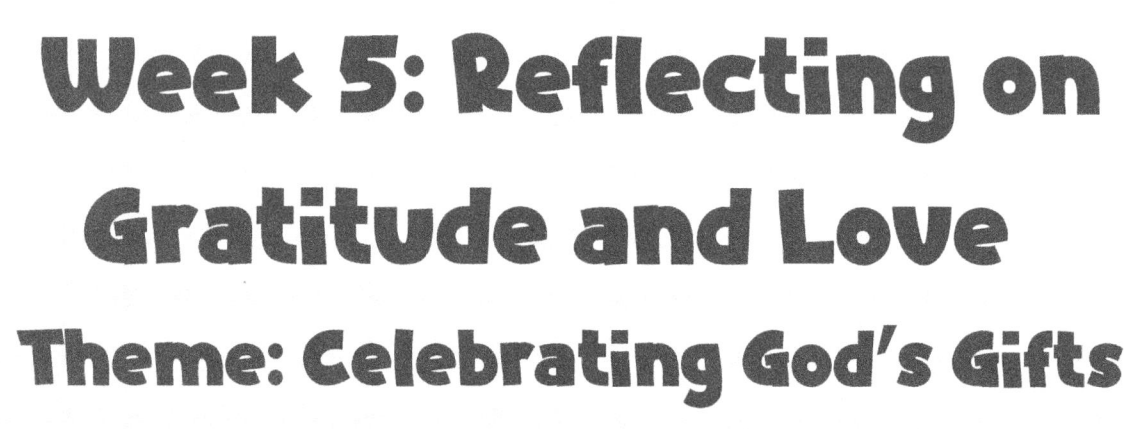

Devotion 17 : The Gift of Life

Scripture: Psalm 139:14

"I praise you because I am fearfully and wonderfully made; your works are wonderful, I know that full well."

Reflection:

Life is a miraculous gift from God. Each day we wake up is an opportunity to celebrate the wonder of creation and the unique way God has designed us. In moments of gratitude, we recognize how precious and extraordinary life truly is. How often do we pause to thank God for the ability to breathe, love, and grow? As you reflect, consider the ways you can cherish this gift and encourage others to do the same.

- **What are some specific ways you can celebrate life daily?**

....

....

....

....

- **How do you share the joy of life with your family?**

....

....

....

....

Prayer:

Dear God, I thank You for the gift of life. Help me to cherish every moment and to live each day with joy and gratitude. May I honor You by using my life to bless others and to reflect Your glory. Amen.

Affirmation:

"I celebrate the gift of life."

Devotion 18 : The Gift of Love

"For God so loved the world that he gave his one and only Son, that whoever believes in him shall not perish but have eternal life."– John 3:16

Reflection:

- *God's love is the ultimate gift—unconditional, eternal, and boundless. This love is the foundation of our faith and the reason we can find hope and joy in all circumstances. Reflecting on God's love reminds us of our worth and encourages us to love others with the same compassion and grace. How can you let God's love shine through you in your relationships, especially with your family?*

- **When have you felt God's love most deeply in your life?**

....

....

....

....

Prayer:

Lord, thank You for the gift of Your love, which sustains me in every moment. Fill my heart and home with Your love, and help me to be a vessel of Your grace and compassion to others. Amen.

Affirmation:

"I embrace God's love in my life."

- **How do you express love to those around you in a way that reflects God's love?**

....

....

....

Devotion 19 : Hope in God's Promises

Scripture :Romans 15:13

"May the God of hope fill you with all joy and peace as you trust in him, so that you may overflow with hope by the power of the Holy Spirit."

Reflection:

- In God's promises, we find hope that strengthens us through life's trials. His promises remind us that we are never alone, that He is faithful, and that His plans for us are good. Trusting in these promises brings joy and peace to our hearts. What are some promises of God that have brought you comfort and hope?

- **Recall a time when God's promises sustained you in a difficult season.**

....

....

....

....

Prayer:

Dear Lord, I thank You for the hope that Your promises provide. Help me to trust in Your plan and to hold onto the joy and peace You offer through Your Word. May I overflow with hope and be a source of encouragement to others. Amen.

Affirmation:

"I carry the hope of God in my heart."

- **How can you share the hope of God's promises with your family?**

....

....

....

....

....

....

Activity for You : Reflecting on Gratitude and Love

Write a journal entry or letter reflecting on the gifts of life, love, and hope that God has given you. Consider including:

- A story about a moment when you felt an overwhelming sense of gratitude for life.
- How you've experienced God's love through your family or personal relationships.
- A time when God's promises gave you hope in a challenging situation.

End your writing with a blessing for your grandchildren, encouraging them to celebrate these gifts and to trust in God's unwavering presence in their lives.

Week 6: Strength Through Challenges

Theme: Finding Resilience in Faith

Devotion 20 : Leaning on God in Difficult Times

Scripture: Psalm 46:1

"God is our refuge and strength, a very present help in trouble."

Reflection:

Life's challenges often feel overwhelming, but God's Word reminds us that we are never alone in our struggles. He is a safe refuge when the storms of life rage, offering protection and strength. When faced with hardships, we can lean into His grace and power, knowing that He is always ready to help. Reflect on moments when God has been your source of strength and how you can turn to Him more fully in times of need.

- **When was the last time you felt God's strength during a tough situation?**

....

....

....

....

- **What practical steps can you take to lean on God's refuge in moments of stress or uncertainty?**

....

....

....

....

Prayer:

Heavenly Father, thank You for being my refuge and source of strength in life's storms. Help me trust You fully and rely on Your guidance when I feel weak. Grant me courage and resilience to face challenges with faith, knowing You are with me always. Amen.

Affirmation:

"I am strong through God's unwavering support."

Devotion 21: Finding Peace Amid Uncertainty

"Fear not, for I am with you; be not dismayed, for I am your God; I will strengthen you, I will help you, I will uphold you with my righteous right hand."– Isaiah 41:10

Reflection:

Uncertainty often leads to fear and anxiety, but God's promise of His constant presence reassures us. He is near, providing strength and upholding us with His love. When we rest in His care, peace replaces fear, and clarity replaces confusion. Think about the uncertainties in your life right now. How can you release those worries to God and trust in His presence to sustain you?

- **What fears or uncertainties are weighing on your heart today?**

....

....

....

....

Prayer:

Lord, thank You for Your unchanging presence in my life. In moments of doubt, help me find peace in Your care and strength in Your love. Teach me to release my fears and trust in Your faithful promises. Amen.

Affirmation:

"I am secure in God's constant presence."

- **How can you remind yourself of God's promise to never leave or forsake you?**

....

....

....

Devotion 22: Trusting God's Timing

Scripture : Ecclesiastes 3:1

"For everything there is a season, and a time for every matter under heaven."

Reflection:

Patience in waiting for God's timing can be difficult, especially when we don't see immediate answers or results. However, God's plans unfold perfectly in His time. Trusting His timing requires surrender and faith, knowing that His vision for our lives is far greater than we can imagine. Consider how waiting has shaped your faith or brought unexpected blessings. What steps can you take to deepen your trust in God's timing, even when answers seem delayed?

- Can you recall a time when waiting on God's timing brought unexpected blessings?

....

....

....

....

Prayer:

Dear Lord, thank You for the assurance that Your timing is perfect. Help me trust in Your plan and grow in patience as I wait for Your will to unfold in my life. Strengthen my faith and grant me peace in the waiting. Amen.

Affirmation:

"I trust God's plan for my life."

How does trusting God's perfect plan give you peace during periods of uncertainty?

....

....

....

....

....

Activity for You : Strength Through Challenges

Write a journal entry or letter reflecting on the strength and resilience God has provided during life's challenges. Consider including:

- A story about a difficult time when you felt God's strength carrying you through and how that experience deepened your faith.
- How God's constant presence has brought you peace during moments of uncertainty or fear.
- A time when trusting in God's timing helped you see His plan unfold in a way that brought clarity and hope.

End your writing with a blessing for your grandchildren, encouraging them to rely on God's strength in their own lives and to trust in His perfect timing, no matter the circumstances.

Week 7 : Passing Down Faith

Theme : Creating a Spiritual Legacy

Devotion 23: Sharing God's Love with the Next Generation

Scripture: Deuteronomy 6:6-7

"These commandments that I give you today are to be on your hearts. Impress them on your children."

Reflection:

As grandparents, you hold a unique role in teaching and modeling faith to the next generation. Reflect on how your words and actions reveal God's love to your family. Sharing stories of God's faithfulness and demonstrating Christ-like values can inspire your grandchildren to seek a relationship with Him. Every conversation, prayer, and moment of kindness sows seeds of spiritual growth in their hearts.

- **How have you shared your faith with your grandchildren in ways that resonate with their unique personalities?**

....

....

....

....

- **What specific steps can you take this week to nurture spiritual conversations with your family?**

....

....

....

Prayer:

"Lord, grant me wisdom and grace to guide my grandchildren in faith. Help me live as an example of Your love and truth, so they may see Your light in my life. Amen."

Affirmation:

"I leave a legacy of love and faith."

Devotion 24 : The Power of a Praying Grandmother

"The prayer of a righteous person is powerful and effective."- James 5:16

Reflection:

Your prayers for your family hold great power. As a grandmother, you are uniquely positioned to intercede for your loved ones, lifting their needs to God. Whether it's for their health, decisions, or spiritual growth, your consistent prayers create a spiritual covering over their lives. Remember, even when you don't see immediate results, your prayers are never in vain; they are treasured by God.

- *What specific concerns or blessings can you bring before God in prayer for each of your grandchildren today?*

....

....

....

....

Prayer:

"Dear Lord, strengthen me to be a prayer warrior for my family. Fill me with faith as I trust You to work in their lives according to Your perfect will. Amen."

Affirmation:

"My prayers uplift and protect my family."

- How can you encourage your grandchildren to build their own prayer habits?

....

....

....

....

Devotion 25 : Planting Seeds of Faith

Scripture : Galatians 6:9

"Let us not become weary in doing good, for at the proper time we will reap a harvest if we do not give up."

Reflection:

- Every small act of faith, love, and encouragement is like planting a seed. You may not always see immediate results, but trust that God will nurture these seeds in His timing. By investing in their spiritual foundation—through scripture, stories, and your example—you create a legacy that will bear fruit in their lives and beyond.

- What "seeds of faith" have you already planted in your family's life, and how can you continue to nurture them?

....

....

....

....

Prayer:

"Lord, help me to persevere in planting seeds of faith. Strengthen my trust in Your timing, and let my love for You shine through all I do for my family. Amen."

Affirmation:

"I plant seeds of faith that will grow for generations."

How has God's timing encouraged you to keep sowing faith, even when results aren't visible?

....

....

....

....

....

....

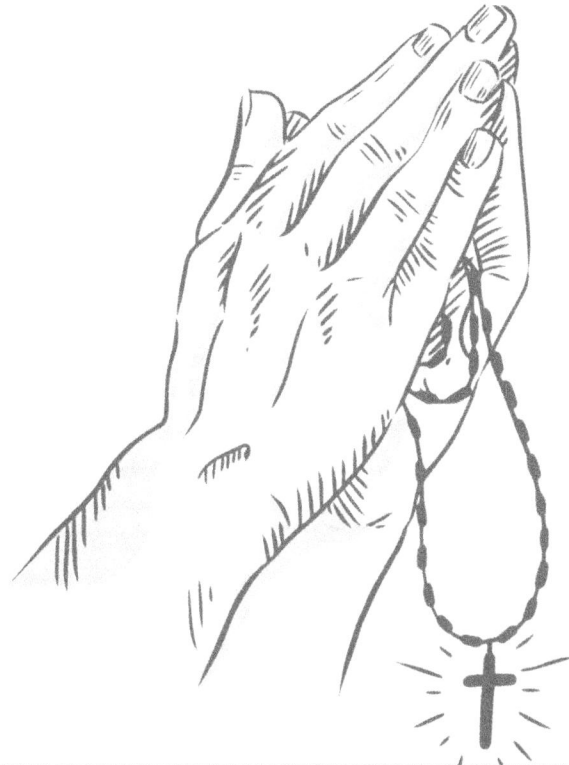

Activity for You : Planting Seeds of Faith

Write a journal entry or letter reflecting on the legacy of faith you wish to leave for your family. Consider including:

- A story about a moment when you shared God's love with your grandchildren.
- How prayer has strengthened your bond with God and your family.
- A time when you trusted God's timing to nurture faith in your loved ones.

End your writing with a blessing for your grandchildren, encouraging them to embrace their own faith journey and trust in God's unfailing love throughout their lives.

Week 8 : Embracing God's Promises

Theme : Living in God's Faithfulness

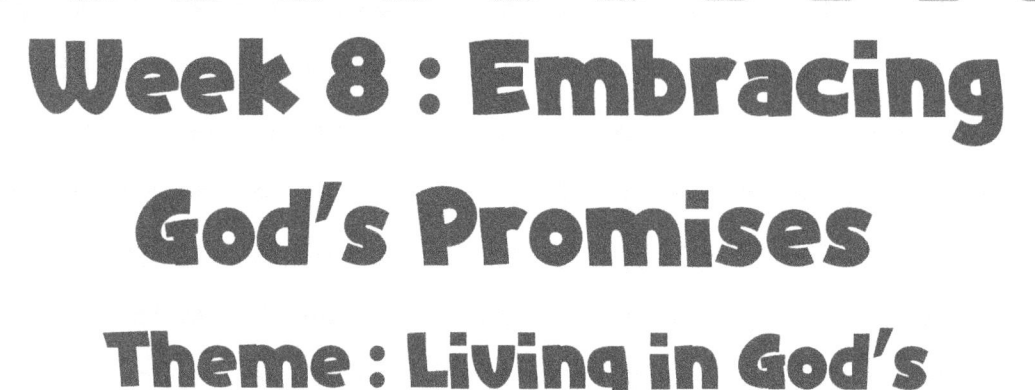

Devotion 26: God's Faithfulness Through Every Season

Scripture: Lamentations 3:22-23

"Because of the Lord's great love we are not consumed, for his compassions never fail. They are new every morning; great is your faithfulness."

Reflection:

Life has its ups and downs, but God's faithfulness remains constant. In every season—whether of joy, sorrow, or uncertainty—God's love and mercy are steadfast. Reflect on the times in your life when God carried you through challenging moments or provided unexpected blessings. His faithfulness reminds us that we are never alone and that His promises endure forever.

- **How has God shown His faithfulness to you in a season of difficulty or change?**

....

....

....

....

- **What steps can you take to remind yourself daily of God's enduring promises?**

....

....

....

Prayer:

"Lord, thank You for Your unchanging faithfulness. Help me to trust in Your compassion and love, no matter the season I face. Amen."

Affirmation:

"I trust in God's faithfulness through all seasons."

Devotion 27: Rejoicing in Eternal Life

"My Father's house has many rooms; if that were not so, would I have told you that I am going there to prepare a place for you? And if I go and prepare a place for you, I will come back and take you to be with me that you also may be where I am." - John 14:2-3

Reflection:

Eternal life is one of God's greatest promises—a gift of hope that transcends the temporary trials of this world. Take comfort in knowing that Jesus has prepared a place for you in His kingdom, where peace and joy abound forever. This assurance allows us to live each day with gratitude and anticipation, knowing our future is secure in His hands.

- **How does the promise of eternal life influence the way you face challenges today?**

Prayer:

"Lord, I thank You for the promise of eternal life. May this hope fill my heart with peace and joy as I live each day for You. Amen."

Affirmation:

"I look forward to the eternal joy God has promised."

- **What can you do to share the hope of God's eternal promise with your family?**

....

....

....

....

Devotion 28: God's Plan for Good

Scripture : Jeremiah 29:11

"For I know the plans I have for you," declares the Lord, "plans to prosper you and not to harm you, plans to give you hope and a future."

Reflection:

God's plans for us are rooted in His perfect love and wisdom. Even when life takes unexpected turns, we can trust that He is working for our good. Reflect on how trusting God's plans has brought peace and clarity to your life. When we align our hearts with His will, we find the strength and courage to move forward with confidence.

- **When has trusting God's plan brought peace or clarity to your life?**

....

....

....

....

Prayer:

"Lord, guide me to walk in the plans You have prepared for me. Help me to trust Your wisdom and to embrace the future with hope. Amen."y. Amen."

Affirmation:

"I walk confidently in the plans God has for me."

- **How can you encourage your family to trust in God's plan for their future?**

....

....

....

....

....

....

....

Activity for You : Embracing God's Promises

Write a journal entry or letter reflecting on how God's promises have brought hope, peace, and purpose to your life. Consider including:

- A story about a time when you experienced God's faithfulness in a challenging season.
- How the promise of eternal life has shaped your perspective on the future.
- A moment when trusting God's plans helped you overcome doubt or fear.

End your writing with a blessing for your grandchildren, encouraging them to trust in God's promises and live with hope and confidence in His faithfulness.

Week 9 : Walking in Obedience

Theme : Aligning Your Life with God's Will

Devotion 29: Listening to God's Voice

- **Scripture: John 10:27**

"My sheep listen to my voice; I know them, and they follow me."

Reflection:

Hearing God's voice requires intentionality. Amid the noise of life, tuning your heart to recognize His gentle whispers is essential. Through prayer, Scripture, and moments of stillness, you can discern His guidance and walk confidently in His will. Ask yourself: Are you making space in your day to listen for God's voice?

- **How do you recognize God's voice in your life? Can you recall a moment when you felt clearly guided by Him?**

....

....

....

....

- **What daily habits can you develop to create more opportunities to hear God's voice?**

....

....

....

Prayer:

Lord, open my ears to hear Your voice clearly. Teach me to recognize Your guidance in my life and to respond with trust and faith. Amen.

Affirmation:

"I listen for God's voice and follow His lead."

Devotion 30: The Blessings of Obedience

"If you fully obey the Lord your God and carefully follow all His commands, the Lord your God will set you high above all the nations on earth. All these blessings will come on you and accompany you if you obey the Lord your God." – Deuteronomy 28:1-2

Reflection:

Obedience opens the door to blessings in every area of life. It's not always easy, but it is always worthwhile. Reflect on the connection between your choices and the blessings you've experienced. Where is God inviting you to walk more fully in obedience?

- **What are some blessings you've received as a result of walking in obedience to God's Word?**

....

....

....

....

Prayer:

Father, thank You for the blessings You pour into my life when I follow Your commands. Strengthen my resolve to align my life with Your Word. Amen.

Affirmation:

"I am blessed as I walk in obedience to God."

- **Are there areas in your life where you're struggling to obey? How can you surrender them to God?**

....

....

....

....

Devotion 31: Trusting in God's Commands

Scripture : Proverbs 3:5-6

"Trust in the Lord with all your heart and lean not on your own understanding; in all your ways submit to Him, and He will make your paths straight."

Reflection:

Trusting God's commands often requires letting go of your own understanding. His ways are higher than ours, and obedience sometimes calls for faith beyond what we can see. What is God asking you to trust Him with today?

- When have you struggled to trust God's plan? How did the situation resolve?

....

....

....

....

Prayer:

Lord, help me trust You with all my heart, even when I don't understand Your ways. Lead me on the path of obedience and faith. Amen.

Affirmation:

"I trust in the Lord and lean on His understanding."

- How can trusting God's commands bring clarity to a decision you are facing?

....

....

....

....

....

....

Devotion 32 : Obedience in Daily Living

- **Scripture: Psalm 119:105**

"Your word is a lamp to my feet, a light on my path."

Reflection:

God's Word is a practical guide for daily life. Every decision, thought, and action can be shaped by His wisdom. Obedience is not just a one-time choice but a daily practice. How can you let God's Word illuminate your path today?

- **What specific verse or passage has guided you recently in making decisions?**

....

....

....

....

....

....

....

....

....

....

Prayer:

God, thank You for Your Word, which lights my way. Help me apply Your truth in every area of my life. Amen.

Affirmation:

"God's Word lights my path as I walk in obedience."

- **How can you incorporate Scripture into your daily routine to help you stay on God's path?**

....

....

....

....

....

....

....

....

....

....

....

Activity for You : Obedience in Daily Living

This week, reflect on your journey of obedience:

- Write a journal entry each day describing how you listened to God's voice and applied His Word.
- Identify one area where you need to trust God more fully and write a prayer surrendering it to Him.
- At the end of the week, summarize the blessings, lessons, or insights you gained through walking in obedience.

Challenge: How has aligning your life with God's will transformed your daily actions and decisions? Write a personal testimony to inspire others.

Week 10: The Power of Forgiveness

Theme: Releasing Burdens Through Grace

Devotion 33: Forgiving as God Forgives

Scripture: Colossians 3:13

"Bear with each other and forgive one another if any of you has a grievance against someone. Forgive as the Lord forgave you."

Reflection:

Forgiveness is at the heart of God's love for us. Jesus' example shows us that forgiveness is not a suggestion but a calling. It can be difficult, but it brings healing and transformation. How can you reflect Christ's forgiveness in your relationships?

- **Is there someone you are struggling to forgive? How does Christ's example inspire you to take the first step?**

....
....
....
....

- **What changes do you notice in your heart and mind when you choose to forgive instead of holding on to resentment?**

....
....
....
....

Prayer:

"Lord, help me to forgive others as You have forgiven me. Fill me with grace and compassion to extend Your love through forgiveness. Amen."

Affirmation:

"I forgive others as God has forgiven me."

Devotion 34: Finding Freedom in Forgiveness

"For if you forgive other people when they sin against you, your heavenly Father will also forgive you. But if you do not forgive others their sins, your Father will not forgive your sins." - Matthew 6:14-15

Reflection:

Forgiveness releases you from the chains of anger and bitterness, allowing peace and joy to flow into your life. Holding onto past hurts weighs you down, but choosing forgiveness opens the door to healing. What burdens are you ready to release today?

- **How has holding onto unforgiveness affected your emotional and spiritual well-being?**

....

....

....

....

Prayer:

"Father, give me the strength to release my pain and let go of the anger in my heart. Help me embrace the freedom and peace that forgiveness brings. Amen."

Affirmation:

"Forgiveness brings peace and freedom to my soul."

- **What steps can you take today to release the burdens of resentment and embrace freedom through forgiveness?**

....

....

....

....

Devotion 35: Restoring Broken Relationships

Scripture : Romans 12:18

"If it is possible, as far as it depends on you, live at peace with everyone." – Romans 12:18

Reflection:

Forgiveness can pave the way to restored relationships. While reconciliation may not always be possible, taking steps toward peace honors God and fosters healing. Are there relationships in your life that need restoration, and how can you initiate the process?

- **Is there a relationship in your life that could benefit from reconciliation? What is one step you can take to restore it?**

....

....

....

....

Prayer:

"Lord, grant me wisdom and courage to take steps toward restoring broken relationships. Help me seek peace and harmony in my interactions with others. Amen.

Affirmation:

"I seek peace and restoration in all my relationships."

- **How does living at peace with others reflect God's love to those around you?**

....

....

....

....

....

....

Activity for You : The Journey of Forgiveness

Reflect on the role of forgiveness in your life:

- Write a letter to someone you are forgiving or to yourself, expressing the freedom and peace that comes with releasing burdens.
- Journal about a time when forgiveness transformed a relationship or healed your heart.
- At the end of the week, write a prayer of gratitude for the healing and blessings that forgiveness has brought into your life.

Challenge: How can your journey of forgiveness inspire others? Write a testimony sharing your experience and how God's grace empowered you to forgive.
:

CONCLUSION

As we come to the close of 10-Week Devotions for Grandma: A Grandma Prayer and Gift Book, may your heart be filled with a sense of purpose, joy, and peace. Over the past ten weeks, you've journeyed through scriptures, prayers, and reflections designed to draw you closer to God and strengthen your role as a grandmother, prayer warrior, and spiritual guide for your family.

Grandmotherhood is a sacred calling, filled with unique opportunities to bless your family and leave a legacy of faith. You've reflected on themes of peace, joy, gratitude, resilience, and obedience, discovering how God's presence can transform every aspect of your life.

Let this be a beginning rather than an end. Take the lessons you've learned, the prayers you've prayed, and the affirmations you've declared, and carry them with you into your daily life. Let them guide your thoughts, shape your actions, and inspire your love for those around you.

A Closing Prayer

Dear Heavenly Father,

Thank You for this journey of devotion, reflection, and growth. Bless every grandmother who has read these words, filling her heart with Your peace, joy, and wisdom. May her life be a testament to Your goodness and grace. Guide her steps as she nurtures her family and shares Your love across generations. May her prayers uplift, her faith inspire, and her presence bring comfort and joy to those she loves. In Jesus' name, Amen.

Final Words

As you continue your journey, remember that your influence as a grandmother extends far beyond what you can see. Every prayer, every word of encouragement, and every act of love leaves an eternal impact. Be bold in your faith, steadfast in your prayers, and joyful in your role.

May God bless you abundantly and keep your heart overflowing with His grace and love. This season of devotion is a joyful reminder that God walks with you every step of the way. You are deeply loved, endlessly cherished, and eternally valued in His sight.

With love and blessings

APPENDIX

Scripture References by Theme

Theme	Scripture Reference	Key Message
Love	1 Corinthians 13:4-7	Love is patient, kind, and enduring.
Faith	Hebrews 11:1	Faith is confidence in what we hope for.
Wisdom	Proverbs 3:5-6	Trust in the Lord and He will guide your paths.
Joy	Nehemiah 8:10	The joy of the Lord is your strength.
Peace	Philippians 4:6-7	God's peace transcends all understanding.
Strength	Isaiah 40:31	Those who hope in the Lord renew their strength.
Forgiveness	Ephesians 4:32	Be kind and forgive, as Christ forgave you.
Gratitude	1 Thessalonians 5:18	Give thanks in all circumstances.
Hope	Romans 15:13	Overflow with hope by the power of the Holy Spirit.
Family Blessings	Psalm 127:3-5	Children are a heritage and reward from the Lord.

Daily Prayer Prompts

Day of the Week	Prayer Focus	Example Prayer Prompt
Monday	Children's Safety	Pray for protection over your grandchildren.
Tuesday	Family Unity	Ask God to strengthen family relationships.
Wednesday	Wisdom for Parents	Pray for your children as they parent.
Thursday	Health and Well-being	Ask for healing and good health for loved ones.
Friday	Spiritual Growth	Pray for your family's deeper walk with God.

APPENDIX

Tips for Leaving a Legacy of Faith

Tip	Practical Application
Share Family Testimonies	Write down and share stories of God's faithfulness.
Teach Scripture Through Stories	Use parables and personal stories to teach lessons.
Model a Prayerful Life	Let your grandchildren see you praying daily.
Give Personalized Blessings	Speak words of encouragement directly to each grandchild.
Celebrate Milestones in Faith	Mark baptisms, confirmations, or spiritual breakthroughs.

We'd Love Your Feedback!

Please let us know how we're doing by leaving us a review.

YOUNG WRITER SERIES - DR. FANATOMY

www.ingramcontent.com/pod-product-compliance
Lightning Source LLC
Chambersburg PA
CBHW082211070526
44585CB00020B/2371